KU-578-892

# Cancer Fighting

## Recipes and Practical Advice for your Health

General Editor: Gina Steer

FLAME TREE
PUBLISHING

**Publisher & Creative Director:** Nick Wells
**Project Editor:** Sarah Goulding
**Designer:** Mike Spender
**With thanks to:** Gina Steer

This is a **FLAME TREE** Book

**FLAME TREE PUBLISHING**
Crabtree Hall, Crabtree Lane
Fulham, London SW6 6TY
United Kingdom
www.flametreepublishing.com

Flame Tree is part of The Foundry Creative Media Company Limited

First published 2005

Copyright © 2005 Flame Tree Publishing

05 07 09 08 06
1 3 5 7 9 10 8 6 4 2

ISBN 1 84451 115 4

All rights reserved. No part of this publication may be reproduced, stored in a retrieval system,
or transmitted in any form or by any means, electronic, mechanical, photocopying, recording or otherwise,
without the prior written permission of the publisher.

A copy of the CIP data for this book is available from the British Library.

Printed in Malaysia

# Contents

# Fighting and Preventing Cancer

**It is an unfortunate fact that cancer is one of the most widespread diseases in the world. A vast amount of research has been done and is still ongoing into both the causes of cancer and what can be done to prevent the outbreak and spread of the disease throughout the body. Although we are still some way off a cure, there have been many breakthroughs over the last 30 years. Scientists now accept that cancer is often hereditary, but current research suggests that a very large contributory factor is lifestyle. With the increase of obesity we are seeing a substantial increase in cancer which can be linked to a bad diet. Other well-documented factors include cigarette smoking, lack of exercise and too much alcohol.**

Cancer can occur in all parts of the body and starts as a rogue cell that gets out of control. Usually the body's immune system controls the growth of cells, but when the immune system breaks down, a 'rogue' cell can occur that starts to behave abnormally. Once the cell goes 'rogue' it can lie undetected for long periods before the growth becomes apparent, but by this time the damage has often been done. The rogue cell spreads throughout the body, embracing and changing healthy cells to form tumours which can either be malignant (that without detection will spread throughout the body) or benign, which grow within themselves.

Preventive measures play a hugely important part in the fight against cancer. There is growing evidence that diet can and does play an important role in both preventing the development of cancer and helping to control it, so it makes sense, especially if you have a family history of cancer, to take note of your diet and if necessary change it.

Food is not only vital as fuel for the body but can also give the immune system that vital boost to help fight the disease. Health experts estimate that roughly one third of all cancers could be diet related. It is strongly advised that, alongside conventional medicine, a healthy diet,

regular exercise and time for relaxation are important factors in both giving yourself the best chance of fighting cancer and improving your quality of life.

In the past, scientists researching cancer-related diseases have been puzzled as to why some countries have a far greater number of cancer sufferers than others. Now that the onset of many cancers have been so strongly linked to diet, it is easier to understand. In the East, where much rice is consumed with very little saturated fat and minimal amounts of meat, there is a far lower incidence of breast, stomach and bowel cancers. Their diet includes a large amount of plant foods containing fibre, as well as very low amounts of the fats and refined products that we eat in the West. The fibre consumed means that the food does not stay in the intestines long and so there is less danger of a build up of toxins.

It therefore makes sense to look carefully at diet in the fight against cancer, whether you are suffering from it or just concerned that you may be at risk. A very simple guide when choosing cancer-fighting foods is to look for the reds, orange and greens and eat plenty of fruit and vegetables. Below are some of the best foods for a cancer-fighting diet in more detail.

**Avacados** are rich in glutathione, a powerful antioxidant that attacks free radicals. Free radicals are naturally produced by the body while producing energy. However if too many free radicals are produced (due to stress, smoking, pollution, the sun rays, illness, etc.) then they can cause cell damage which leads to cancer and other diseases. Avocados also provide more potassium than bananas and are a strong source of beta carotene.

**Broccoli, Brussels sprouts, cabbage and cauliflower** have a chemical component called indole-3-carbinol that can help combat breast cancer. Broccoli also contains the phytochemical sulforaphane, believed to help prevent colon and rectal cancer. All contain antioxidants that may help decrease prostate and other cancers.

**Carrots** also contain large amounts of beta carotene, which may help reduce a wide range of cancers. Falcarinol, also found in carrots, is thought to reduce the risk of developing the disease. They are best eaten raw for the most benefit.

**Chilli peppers** contain capsaicin, which may neutralize certain cancer-causing substances and help prevent stomach cancer.

**Fish and shellfish**, especially oily fish, rich in omega 3 fatty acids, should be eaten two to three times a week. Fish contains selenium as well as having no saturated fat.

**Fruit** is hugely important to any healthy diet, but particularly one that aims to fight cancer. Figs, grapefruit, oranges, lemons, grapes, papayas and all berries (especially raspberries, strawberries, blueberries and blackberries) should all be eaten regularly.

**Garlic** has immune-enhancing allium compounds that appear to increase the activity of immune cells that fight cancer and indirectly help break down cancer-causing substances. Onions, leeks and chives are good to include in your diet for the same reason.

**Mushrooms** appear to help the body fight cancer and build the immune system. They contain polysaccharides that build immunity and a protein called lectin, which attacks cancerous cells and prevents them from multiplying.

**Nuts** contain antioxidants and selenium, both of which are important in fighting cancer.

**Soya products** such as tofu contain several types of phytoestrogens that could help prevent both breast and prostate cancers by blocking and suppressing cancerous changes.

**Sweet potatoes** have many anti-cancer properties including beta carotene.

**Tomatoes** are also antioxidant-rich and contain plenty of vitamin C, which can prevent the cellular damage that leads to cancer. Watermelons, carrots and red peppers also contain these substances, but in lesser quantities.

There are some foods that should be avoided when following a cancer-fighting diet, or a healthy diet generally. Exclude all refined products such as biscuits, cakes, white breads and sugar-coated cereals. This will greatly help to reduce obesity, a contributory factor, and detox your body. Smoked, salt cured and pickled foods should also be avoided. Alcohol should be limited, but red wine contains powerful antioxidants called polyphenols that may protect against various types of cancer. However, alcohol can be toxic to the liver and nervous system, and some research has indicated that it may be a carcinogen. 'All things in moderation' should perhaps be your guide here.

This book has been specifically designed to offer a range of recipes featuring some of the best cancer-fighting foods, whether you have cancer and want to do all you can to beat it, or you are concerned that you may be at risk in the future. With delicious recipes such as Carrot & Ginger Soup, Citrus-grilled Plaice and Italian Baked Tomatoes, there is something here for everyone.

# Baked Macaroni with Mushrooms & Leeks

## Nutritional details

### per 100 g

| | |
|---|---|
| energy | 111 kcals/461 kj |
| protein | 3 g |
| carbohydrate | 10 g |
| fat | 7 g |
| fibre | 0.9 g |
| sugar | 1.9 g |
| sodium | 0.1 g |

## Ingredients    Serves 4

2 tbsp olive oil
1 onion, peeled and finely chopped
1 garlic clove, peeled and crushed
2 small leeks, trimmed
    and chopped
450 g/1 lb assorted wild
    mushrooms, trimmed
50 ml/2 fl oz white wine
75 g/3 oz butter
150 ml/¼ pint crème fraîche
    or whipping cream
salt and freshly ground
    black pepper
75 g/3 oz fresh white breadcrumbs
350 g/12 oz short cut macaroni
1 tbsp freshly chopped parsley,
    to garnish

## Step-by-step guide

1  Preheat the oven to 220°C/ 425°F/Gas Mark 7, 15 minutes before cooking. Heat 1 tablespoon of the olive oil in a large frying pan, add the onion and garlic and cook for 2 minutes. Add the leeks, mushrooms and 25 g/1 oz of the butter then cook for 5 minutes. Pour in the white wine, cook for 2 minutes then stir in the crème fraîche or cream. Season to taste with salt and pepper.

2  Meanwhile, bring a large pan of lightly salted water to a rolling boil. Add the macaroni and cook according to the packet instructions, or until 'al dente'.

3  Melt 25 g/1 oz of the butter with the remaining oil in a small frying pan. Add the breadcrumbs and fry until just beginning to turn golden brown. Drain on absorbent kitchen paper.

4  Drain the pasta thoroughly, toss in the remaining butter then tip into a lightly oiled, 1.4 litre/2½ pint shallow baking dish. Cover the pasta with the leek and mushroom mixture then sprinkle with the fried breadcrumbs. Bake in the preheated oven for 5–10 minutes, or until golden and crisp. Garnish with chopped parsley and serve.

✓ cows' milk-free    ✓ egg-free    ✓ gluten-free    ✓ wheat-free    ✓ nut-free    ✓ vegetarian    ✓ vegan    ✓ seafood-free

# Beef Fajitas with Avocado Sauce

## Nutritional details

### per 100 g

| | |
|---|---|
| energy | 177 kcals/740 kj |
| protein | 11 g |
| carbohydrate | 16 g |
| fat | 8 g |
| fibre | 1.2 g |
| sugar | 1.4 g |
| sodium | 0.2 g |

## Ingredients     Serves 3–6

2 tbsp sunflower oil
450 g/1 lb beef fillet or
    rump steak, trimmed
    and cut into thin strips
2 garlic cloves, peeled
    and crushed
1 tsp ground cumin
¼ tsp cayenne pepper
1 tbsp paprika
230 g can chopped tomatoes
215 g can red kidney beans, drained
1 tbsp freshly chopped coriander
1 avocado, peeled, pitted
    and chopped
1 shallot, peeled and chopped
1 large tomato, skinned,
    deseeded and chopped
1 red chilli, diced
1 tbsp lemon juice
6 large flour tortilla pancakes
3–4 tbsp soured cream
green salad, to serve

## Step-by-step guide

1   Heat the wok, add the oil, then stir-fry the beef for 3–4 minutes. Add the garlic and spices and continue to cook for a further 2 minutes. Stir the tomatoes into the wok, bring to the boil, cover and simmer gently for 5 minutes.

2   Meanwhile, blend the kidney beans in a food processor until slightly broken up, then add to the wok. Continue to cook for a further 5 minutes, adding 2–3 tablespoons of water. The mixture should be thick and fairly dry. Stir in the chopped coriander.

3   Mix the chopped avocado, shallot, tomato, chilli and lemon juice together. Spoon into a serving dish and reserve.

4   When ready to serve, warm the tortillas and spread with a little soured cream. Place a spoonful of the beef mixture on top, followed by a spoonful of the avocado sauce, then roll up. Repeat until all the mixture is used up. Serve immediately with a green salad.

cows' milk-free  egg-free  gluten-free  wheat-free  nut-free  vegetarian  vegan  seafood-free

# Bruschetta with Pecorino, Garlic & Tomatoes

## Nutritional details

### per 100 g

| | |
|---|---|
| energy | 152 kcals/632 kj |
| protein | 8 g |
| carbohydrate | 6 g |
| fat | 11 g |
| fibre | 1.2 g |
| sugar | 2.6 g |
| sodium | 0.2 g |

## Ingredients          Serves 4

6 ripe but firm tomatoes
125 g/4 oz pecorino cheese,
    finely grated
1 tbsp oregano leaves
salt and freshly ground
    black pepper
3 tbsp olive oil
3 garlic cloves, peeled
8 slices of flat Italian bread,
    such as focaccia
50 g/2 oz mozzarella cheese
marinated black olives, to serve

## Step-by-step guide

1  Preheat the grill and line the grill rack with tinfoil just before cooking. Make a small cross in the top of the tomatoes, then place in a small bowl and cover with boiling water. Leave to stand for 2 minutes, then drain and remove the skins. Cut into quarters, remove the seeds, and chop the flesh into small dice.

2  Mix the tomato flesh with the pecorino cheese and 2 teaspoons of the fresh oregano and season to taste with salt and pepper. Add 1 tablespoon of the olive oil and mix thoroughly.

3  Crush the garlic and spread evenly over the slices of bread. Heat 2 tablespoons of the olive oil in a large frying pan and sauté the bread slices until they are crisp and golden.

4  Place the fried bread on a lightly oiled baking tray and spoon on the tomato and cheese topping. Put a little mozzarella on top and place under the preheated grill for 3–4 minutes, until golden and bubbling. Garnish with the remaining oregano, then arrange the bruschettas on a serving plate and serve immediately with the olives.

✓ cows' milk-free   ✓ egg-free   ✓ gluten-free   ✓ wheat-free   ✓ nut-free   ✓ vegetarian   ✓ vegan   ✓ seafood-free

# Cabbage Timbale

## Nutritional details

### per 100 g

| | |
|---|---|
| energy | 89 kcals/373 kj |
| protein | 5 g |
| carbohydrate | 8 g |
| fat | 5 g |
| fibre | 2.4 g |
| sugar | 2.7 g |
| sodium | 0.3 g |

## Ingredients    Serves 4–6

1 small savoy cabbage,
   weighing about 350 g/12 oz
salt and freshly ground black pepper
2 tbsp olive oil
1 leek, trimmed and chopped
1 garlic clove, peeled and crushed
75 g/3 oz long-grain rice
200 g can chopped tomatoes
300 ml/½ pint vegetable stock
400 g can flageolet beans,
   drained and rinsed
75 g/3 oz Cheddar cheese,grated
1 tbsp freshly chopped oregano

**To garnish:**
Greek yogurt with paprika
tomato wedges

## Step-by-step guide

1   Preheat the oven to 180°C/350°F/
Gas Mark 4, 10 minutes before
required. Remove six of the outer
leaves of the cabbage. Cut off the
thickest part of the stalk and
blanch the leaves in lightly salted
boiling water for 2 minutes. Lift out
with a slotted spoon and briefly
rinse under cold water and reserve.

2   Remove the stalks from the rest of
the cabbage leaves. Shred the
leaves and blanch in the boiling
water for 1 minute. Drain, rinse
under cold water and pat
dry on absorbent kitchen paper.

3   Heat the oil in a frying pan
and cook the leek and garlic
for 5 minutes. Stir in the rice,
chopped tomatoes with their juice
and the stock. Bring to the boil,
cover and simmer for 15 minutes.

4   Remove the lid and simmer for a
further 4–5 minutes, stirring
frequently, until the liquid is
absorbed and the rice is tender.
Stir in the flageolet beans, cheese
and oregano. Season to taste with
salt and pepper.

5   Line an oiled 1.1 litre/2 pint
pudding basin with some of the
large cabbage leaves, overlapping
them slightly. Fill the basin with
alternate layers of rice mixture
and shredded leaves, pressing
down well.

6   Cover the top with the remaining
leaves. Cover with oiled tinfoil
and bake in the preheated for
30 minutes. Leave to stand for
10 minutes. Turn out, cut into
wedges and serve with yogurt
sprinkled with paprika and
tomato wedges.

cows' milk-free   egg-free   gluten-free   wheat-free   nut-free   vegetarian   vegan   seafood-free

9

# Carrot & Ginger Soup

## Nutritional details

### per 100 g

| | |
|---|---|
| energy | 75 kcals/314 kj |
| protein | 3 g |
| carbohydrate | 13 g |
| fat | 2 g |
| fibre | 2 g |
| sugar | 4.3 g |
| sodium | 0.5 g |

## Ingredients          Serves 4

4 slices of bread,
    crusts removed
1 tsp yeast extract
2 tsp olive oil
1 onion, peeled and chopped
1 garlic clove,
    peeled and crushed
½ tsp ground ginger
450 g/1 lb carrots,
    peeled and chopped
1 litre/1¾ pint vegetable stock
2.5 cm/1 inch piece of
    root ginger, peeled and
    finely grated
salt and freshly ground
    black pepper
1 tbsp lemon juice

**To garnish:**
chives
lemon zest

## Step-by-step guide

1  Preheat the oven to 180°C/350°F/ Gas Mark 4. Roughly chop the bread. Dissolve the yeast extract in 2 tablespoons of warm water and mix with the bread.

2  Spread the bread cubes over a lightly oiled baking tray and bake for 20 minutes, turning halfway through. Remove from the oven and reserve.

3  Heat the oil in a large saucepan. Gently cook the onion and garlic for 3–4 minutes.

4  Stir in the ground ginger and cook for 1 minute to release the flavour.

5  Add the chopped carrots, then stir in the stock and the fresh ginger. Simmer gently for 15 minutes.

6  Remove from the heat and allow to cool a little. Blend until smooth, then season to taste with salt and pepper. Stir in the lemon juice. Garnish with the chives and lemon zest and serve immediately.

cows' milk-free · egg-free · gluten-free · wheat-free · nut-free · vegetarian · vegan · seafood-free

# Chicken & New Potatoes on Rosemary Skewers

## Nutritional details

### per 100 g

| | |
|---|---|
| energy | 113 kcals/478 kj |
| protein | 10 g |
| carbohydrate | 13 g |
| fat | 3 g |
| fibre | 0.6 g |
| sugar | 1.1 g |
| sodium | trace |

## Ingredients          Serves 4

8 thick fresh rosemary stems,
    at least 23 cm/9 inches long
3–4 tbsp extra virgin olive oil
2 garlic cloves, peeled and crushed
1 tsp freshly chopped thyme
grated rind and juice of 1 lemon
salt and freshly ground black pepper
4 skinless chicken breast fillets
16 small new potatoes,
    peeled or scrubbed
8 very small onions or shallots, peeled
1 large yellow or red pepper, deseeded
lemon wedges, to garnish
freshly cooked couscous, to serve

## Step-by-step guide

1   Preheat the grill and line the grill rack with tinfoil just before cooking. If using a barbecue, light it at least 20 minutes before required. Strip the leaves from the rosemary stems, leaving about 5 cm/2 inches of soft leaves at the top. Chop the leaves coarsely and reserve. Using a sharp knife, cut the thicker, woody ends of the stems to a point that can pierce the chicken pieces and potatoes. Blend the chopped rosemary, oil, garlic, thyme and lemon rind and juice in a shallow dish. Season to taste with salt and pepper.

2   Cut the chicken into 4 cm/½ inch cubes, add to the oil and stir well. Cover and refrigerate for at least 30 minutes, turning occasionally.

3   Cook the potatoes in lightly salted boiling water for 10–12 minutes until just tender. Add the onions to the potatoes 2 minutes before the end of the cooking time. Drain, rinse under cold running water and leave to cool. Cut the pepper into 2.5 cm/1 inch squares.

4   Beginning with a piece of chicken and starting with the pointed end of the skewer, alternately thread equal amounts of chicken, potato, pepper and onion onto each rosemary skewer. Cover the leafy ends of the skewers with tinfoil to stop them from burning. Do not thread the chicken and vegetables too closely together on the skewer or the chicken may not cook completely.

5   Cook the kebabs for 15 minutes, or until tender and golden, turning and brushing with either extra oil or the marinade. Remove the tinfoil, garnish with lemon wedges and serve on couscous.

✓ cows' milk-free   ✓ egg-free   ✓ gluten-free   ✓ wheat-free   ✓ nut-free   ✓ vegetarian   ✓ vegan   ✓ seafood-free

# Chicken Pie with Sweet Potato Topping

## Nutritional details

### per 100 g

| | |
|---|---|
| energy | 96 kcals/405 kj |
| protein | 7 g |
| carbohydrate | 11 g |
| fat | 3 g |
| fibre | 0.5 g |
| sugar | 0.9 g |
| sodium | 0.1 g |

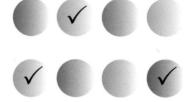

## Ingredients          Serves 4

700 g/1½ lb sweet potatoes,
    peeled and cut into chunks
salt and freshly ground black pepper
250 g/9 oz potatoes,
    peeled and cut into chunks
150 ml/¼ pint milk
25 g/1 oz butter
2 tsp brown sugar
grated rind of 1 orange
4 skinless chicken breast
    fillets, diced
1 medium onion, peeled and
    coarsely chopped
125 g/4 oz baby mushrooms,
    stems trimmed
2 leeks, trimmed and thickly sliced
150 ml/¼ pint dry white wine
1 chicken stock cube
1 tbsp freshly chopped parsley
50 ml/2 fl oz crème fraîche
    or thick double cream
green vegetables, to serve

## Step-by-step guide

1   Preheat the oven to 190°C/
    375°F/Gas Mark 5, 10 minutes
    before required. Cook the
    potatoes in lightly salted boiling
    water until tender. Drain well, then
    return to the saucepan and mash
    until smooth and creamy,
    gradually adding the milk, then
    the butter, sugar and orange rind.
    Season to taste with salt and
    pepper and reserve.

2   Place the chicken in a saucepan
    with the onion, mushrooms,
    leeks, wine, stock cube and
    season to taste. Simmer, covered,
    until the chicken and vegetables
    are tender. Using a slotted spoon,
    transfer the chicken and
    vegetables to a 1.1 litre/2 pint pie
    dish. Add the parsley and crème
    fraîche or cream to the liquid in
    the pan and bring to the boil.
    Simmer until thickened and
    smooth, stirring constantly. Pour
    over the chicken in the pie dish,
    mix and cool.

3   Spread the mashed potato over
    the chicken filling, and swirl the
    surface into decorative peaks.
    Bake in the preheated oven for
    35 minutes, or until the top is
    golden and the chicken filling
    is heated through. Serve
    immediately with fresh
    green vegetables.

✓ cows' milk-free   ✓ egg-free   ✓ gluten-free   ✓ wheat-free   ✓ nut-free   ✓ vegetarian   ✓ vegan   ✓ seafood-free

# Citrus-grilled Plaice

## Nutritional details

### per 100 g

| | |
|---|---|
| energy | 74 kcals/312 kj |
| protein | 8 g |
| carbohydrate | 8 g |
| fat | 1 g |
| fibre | 0.4 g |
| sugar | 1.4 g |
| sodium | 0.2 g |

## Ingredients          Serves 4

1 tsp sunflower oil
1 onion, peeled and chopped
1 orange pepper,
    deseeded and chopped
175 g/6 oz long-grain rice
150 ml/¼ pint orange juice
2 tbsp lemon juice
225 ml/8 fl oz vegetable stock
spray of oil
4 x 175 g/6 oz plaice
    fillets, skinned
1 orange
1 lemon
25 g/1 oz half-fat butter
    or low fat spread
2 tbsp freshly chopped tarragon
salt and freshly ground
    black pepper
lemon wedges,
    to garnish

## Step-by-step guide

1  Heat the oil in a large frying pan, then sauté the onion, pepper and rice for 2 minutes.

2  Add the orange and lemon juice and bring to the boil. Reduce the heat, add half the stock and simmer for 15–20 minutes, or until the rice is tender, adding the remaining stock as necessary.

3  Preheat the grill. Finely spray the base of the grill pan with oil. Place the plaice fillets in the base and reserve.

4  Finely grate the orange and lemon rind. Squeeze the juice from half of each fruit.

5  Melt the butter or low-fat spread in a small saucepan. Add the grated rind, juice and half of the tarragon and use to baste the plaice fillets.

6  Cook one side only of the fish under the preheated grill at a medium heat for 4–6 minutes, basting continuously.

7  Once the rice is cooked, stir in the remaining tarragon and season to taste with salt and pepper. Garnish the fish with the lemon wedges and serve immediately with the rice.

cows' milk-free    egg-free    gluten-free    wheat-free    nut-free    vegetarian    vegan    seafood-free

# Creamy Vegetable Korma

## Nutritional details

### per 100 g

| | |
|---|---|
| energy | 133 kcals/557 kj |
| protein | 3 g |
| carbohydrate | 17 g |
| fat | 6 g |
| fibre | 1.7 g |
| sugar | 2.7 g |
| sodium | 0.3 g |

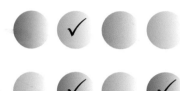

## Ingredients     Serves 4-6

2 tbsp ghee or vegetable oil
1 large onion, peeled and chopped
2 garlic cloves, peeled and crushed
2.5 cm/1 inch piece of root ginger,
      peeled and grated
4 cardamom pods
2 tsp ground coriander
1 tsp ground cumin
1 tsp ground turmeric
finely grated rind and juice
      of ½ lemon
50 g/2 oz ground almonds
400 ml/14 fl oz vegetable stock
450 g/1 lb potatoes, peeled
      and diced
450 g/1 lb mixed vegetables,
      such as cauliflower, carrots
      and turnip, cut into chunks
150 ml/¼ pint double cream
3 tbsp freshly chopped coriander
salt and freshly ground
      black pepper
naan bread, to serve

## Step-by-step guide

1   Heat the ghee or oil in a large saucepan. Add the onion and cook for 5 minutes. Stir in the garlic and ginger and cook for a further 5 minutes, or until soft and just beginning to colour.

2   Stir in the cardamom, ground coriander, cumin and turmeric. Continue cooking over a low heat for 1 minute, stirring.

3   Stir in the lemon rind and juice and almonds. Blend in the vegetable stock. Slowly bring to the boil, stirring occasionally.

4   Add the potatoes and vegetables. Bring back to the boil, then reduce the heat, cover and simmer for 35–40 minutes, or until the vegetables are just tender. Check after 25 minutes and add a little more stock if needed.

5   Slowly stir in the cream and chopped coriander. Season to taste with salt and pepper. Cook very gently until heated through, but do not boil. Serve immediately with naan bread.

✔ cows' milk-free   ✔ egg-free   ✔ gluten-free   ✔ wheat-free   • nut-free   ✔ vegetarian   • vegan   ✔ seafood-free

# Fruity Rice-stuffed Poussins

## Nutritional details

### per 100 g

| | |
|---|---|
| energy | 186 kcals/778 kj |
| protein | 10 g |
| carbohydrate | 18 g |
| fat | 8 g |
| fibre | 0.9 g |
| sugar | 8.8 g |
| sodium | 0.1 g |

## Ingredients　　Serves 6

**For the rice stuffing:**
225 ml/8 fl oz port
125 g/4 oz raisins
125 g/4 oz ready-to-eat dried
　apricots, chopped
2 tbsp olive oil
1 medium onion,
　peeled and finely chopped
1 celery stalk,
　trimmed and finely sliced
2 garlic cloves,
　peeled and finely chopped
1½ tsp mixed spice
1 tsp each dried oregano and
　mint or basil
225 g/8 oz unsweetened canned
　chestnuts, chopped
200 g/7 oz long-grain white
　rice, cooked
grated rind and juice of 2 oranges
350 ml/12 fl oz chicken stock
50 g/2 oz walnut halves, lightly
　toasted and chopped
2 tbsp each freshly chopped

mint and parsley
salt and freshly ground black pepper
6 oven-ready poussins
50 g/2 oz butter, melted

**To garnish:**
fresh herbs
orange wedges

---

## Step-by-step guide

1　Preheat the oven to 180°C/
　350°F/Gas Mark 4. To make the
　stuffing, place the port, raisins
　and apricots in a bowl and leave
　for 15 minutes. Heat the oil in a
　large saucepan. Add the onion
　and celery and cook for 3–4
　minutes. Add the garlic, mixed
　spice, herbs and chestnuts and
　cook for 4 minutes, stirring
　occasionally. Add the rice, half the
　orange rind and juice and the
　stock. Simmer for 5 minutes until
　most of the liquid is absorbed.

2　Drain the raisins and apricots,
　reserving the port. Stir into the
　rice with the walnuts, mint,
　parsley and seasoning and cook
　for 2 minutes. Remove and cool.

3　Rinse the poussin cavities, pat dry
　and season with salt and pepper.
　Lightly fill the cavities with the
　stuffing. Tie the poussins' legs
　together, tucking in the tail. Form
　any extra stuffing into balls.

4　Place in roasting tins with stuffing
　balls and brush with melted
　butter. Drizzle over the remaining
　butter, remaining orange rind and
　juice and port. Roast in the
　preheated oven for 50 minutes or
　until golden and cooked, basting
　every 15 minutes. Transfer to a
　platter, cover with tinfoil and rest.
　Pour over any pan juices. Garnish
　with herbs and orange wedges
　and serve with the stuffing.

# Fusilli Pasta with Spicy Tomato Salsa

## Nutritional details

### per 100 g

| | |
|---|---|
| energy | 59 kcals/252 kj |
| protein | 3 g |
| carbohydrate | 12 g |
| fat | 0.7 g |
| fibre | 0.6 g |
| sugar | 0.3 g |
| sodium | trace |

## Ingredients     Serves 4

6 large ripe tomatoes
2 tbsp lemon juice
2 tbsp lime juice
grated rind of 1 lime
2 shallots, peeled and
    finely chopped
2 garlic cloves, peeled
    and finely chopped
1–2 red chillies
1–2 green chillies
450 g/1 lb fresh fusilli pasta
4 tbsp half-fat crème fraîche
2 tbsp freshly chopped basil
sprig of oregano, to garnish

---

## Step-by-step guide

1 Place the tomatoes in a bowl and cover with boiling water. Allow to stand until the skins start to peel away.

2 Remove the skins from the tomatoes, divide each tomato in four and remove all the seeds. Chop the flesh into small cubes and put in a small pan. Add the lemon and lime juice and the grated lime rind and stir well.

3 Add the chopped shallots and garlic. Remove the seeds carefully from the chillies, chop finely and add to the pan.

4 Bring to the boil and simmer gently for 5–10 minutes until the salsa has thickened slightly.

5 Reserve the salsa to allow the flavours to develop while the pasta is cooking.

6 Bring a large pan of water to the boil and add the pasta. Simmer gently for 3–4 minutes or until the pasta is just tender.

7 Drain the pasta and rinse in boiling water. Top with a large spoonful of salsa and a small spoonful of crème fraîche. Garnish with the chopped basil and oregano and serve immediately.

cows' milk-free   egg-free   gluten-free   wheat-free   nut-free   vegetarian   vegan   seafood-free

# Gnocchetti with Broccoli & Bacon Sauce

## Nutritional details

### per 100 g

| | |
|---|---|
| energy | 133 kcals/556 kj |
| protein | 6 g |
| carbohydrate | 13 g |
| fat | 7 g |
| fibre | 1.6 g |
| sugar | 1.4 g |
| sodium | 0.2 g |

## Ingredients   Serves 6

450 g/1 lb broccoli florets
4 tbsp olive oil
50 g/2 oz pancetta
   or smoked bacon,
   finely chopped
1 small onion, peeled and
   finely chopped
3 garlic cloves,
   peeled and sliced
200 ml/7 fl oz milk
450 g/1 lb gnocchetti
   (little elongated
   ribbed shells)
50 g/2 oz freshly grated
   Parmesan cheese,
   plus extra to serve
salt and freshly ground
   black pepper

## Step-by-step guide

1. Bring a large pan of salted water to the boil. Add the broccoli florets and cook for about 8–10 minutes, or until very soft. Drain thoroughly, allow to cool slightly then chop finely and reserve.

2. Heat the olive oil in a heavy-based pan, add the pancetta or bacon and cook over a medium heat for 5 minutes, or until golden and crisp. Add the onion and cook for a further 5 minutes, or until soft and lightly golden. Add the garlic and cook for 1 minute.

3. Transfer the chopped broccoli to the bacon or pancetta mixture and pour in the milk. Bring slowly to the boil and simmer rapidly for about 15 minutes, or until reduced to a creamy texture.

4. Meanwhile, bring a large pan of lightly salted water to a rolling boil. Add the pasta and cook according to the packet instructions, or until 'al dente'.

5. Drain the pasta thoroughly, reserving a little of the cooking water. Add the pasta and the Parmesan cheese to the broccoli mixture. Toss, adding enough of the reserved cooking water to make a creamy sauce. Season to taste with salt and pepper. Serve immediately with extra Parmesan cheese.

cows' milk-free   egg-free   gluten-free   wheat-free   nut-free   vegetarian   vegan   seafood-free

# Herbed Hasselback Potatoes with Roast Chicken

## Nutritional details

### per 100 g

| | |
|---|---|
| energy | 98 kcals/412 kj |
| protein | 6 g |
| carbohydrate | 10 g |
| fat | 4 g |
| fibre | 1.7 g |
| sugar | 1.8 g |
| sodium | trace |

## Ingredients        Serves 4

8 medium, evenly-sized
    potatoes, peeled
3 large sprigs of fresh rosemary
1 tbsp oil
salt and freshly ground black pepper
350 g/12 oz baby parsnips, peeled
350 g/12 oz baby carrots, peeled
350 g/12 oz baby leeks, trimmed
75 g/3 oz butter
finely grated rind of 1 lemon,
    preferably unwaxed
1.6 kg/3½ lb chicken

## Step-by-step guide

1   Preheat the oven to 200°C/400°F/
Gas Mark 6, about 15 minutes
before cooking. Place a chopstick
on either side of a potato and, with
a sharp knife, cut down through
the potato until you reach the
chopsticks; take care not to cut
right through the potato. Repeat
these cuts every 5 mm/¼ inch
along the length of the potato.
Carefully ease 2–4 of the slices
apart and slip in a few rosemary
sprigs. Repeat with remaining
potatoes. Brush with the oil and
season well with salt and pepper.

2   Place the seasoned potatoes in
a large roasting tin. Add the
parsnips, carrots and leeks
to the potatoes in the tin and
cover with a wire rack or trivet.

3   Beat the butter and lemon rind
together and season to taste.
Smear the chicken with the lemon
butter and place on the rack over
the vegetables.

4   Roast in the preheated oven
for 1 hour 40 minutes, basting
the chicken and vegetables
occasionally, until cooked
thoroughly. The juices should
run clear when the thigh is
pierced with a skewer. Place
the cooked chicken on a warmed
serving platter, arrange the
roast vegetables around it
and serve immediately.

✓ cows' milk-free    ✓ egg-free    ✓ gluten-free    ✓ wheat-free    ✓ nut-free    ✓ vegetarian    ✓ vegan    ✓ seafood-free

# Hot Herby Mushrooms

## Nutritional details

### per 100 g

| | |
|---|---|
| energy | 81 kcals/342 kj |
| protein | 4 g |
| carbohydrate | 15 g |
| fat | 1 g |
| fibre | 0.7 g |
| sugar | 1.8 g |
| sodium | 0.5 g |

## Ingredients        Serves 4

4 thin slices of white bread,
   crusts removed
125 g/4 oz chestnut mushrooms,
   wiped and sliced
125 g/4 oz oyster
   mushrooms, wiped
1 garlic clove, peeled and crushed
1 tsp Dijon mustard
300 ml/½ pint vegetable stock
 salt and freshly ground
   black pepper
1 tbsp freshly chopped parsley
1 tbsp freshly snipped chives,
   plus extra to garnish
mixed salad leaves, to serve

## Step-by-step guide

1  Preheat the oven to 180°C/
   350°F/Gas Mark 4. With a rolling
   pin, roll each piece of bread out
   as thinly as possible.

2  Press each piece of bread into a
   10 cm/4 inch tartlet tin. Push each
   piece firmly down, then bake in the
   preheated oven for 20 minutes.

3  Place the mushrooms in a frying
   pan with the garlic, mustard and
   chicken stock and stir-fry over a
   moderate heat until the
   mushrooms are tender and the
   liquid is reduced by half.

4  Carefully remove the mushrooms
   from the frying pan with a slotted
   spoon and transfer to a heat-
   resistant dish. Cover with tinfoil
   and place in the bottom of the oven
   to keep the mushrooms warm.

5  Boil the remaining pan juices until
   reduced to a thick sauce. Season
   with salt and pepper.

6  Stir the parsley and the chives into
   the mushroom mixture.

7  Place one bread tartlet case on each
   plate and divide the mushroom
   mixture between them.

8  Spoon over the pan juices,
   garnish with the chives and
   serve immediately with mixed
   salad leaves.

# Indonesian Salad with Peanut Dressing

## Nutritional details

### per 100 g

| | |
|---|---|
| energy | 134 kcals/560 kj |
| protein | 6 g |
| carbohydrate | 8 g |
| fat | 9 g |
| fibre | 1.3 g |
| sugar | 2.1 g |
| sodium | 0.2 g |

## Ingredients      Serves 4

225 g/8 oz new potatoes, scrubbed
1 large carrot, peeled and
    cut into matchsticks
125 g/4 oz French beans, trimmed
225 g/8 oz tiny cauliflower florets
125 g/4 oz cucumber,
    cut into matchsticks
75 g/3 oz fresh bean sprouts
3 medium eggs, hard-boiled
    and quartered

**For the peanut dressing:**
2 tbsp sesame oil
1 garlic clove, peeled and crushed
1 red chilli, deseeded and
    finely chopped
150 g/5 oz crunchy peanut butter
6 tbsp hot vegetable stock
2 tsp soft light brown sugar
2 tsp dark soy sauce
1 tbsp lime juice

## Step-by-step guide

1  Cook the potatoes in a saucepan of boiling salted water for 15–20 minutes until tender. Remove with a slotted spoon and thickly slice into a large bowl. Keep the saucepan of water boiling.

2  Add the carrot, French beans and cauliflower to the water, return to the boil and cook for 2 minutes, or until just tender. Drain and refresh under cold running water, then drain well. Add to the potatoes with the cucumber and bean sprouts.

3  To make the dressing, gently heat the sesame oil in a small saucepan. Add the garlic and chilli and cook for a few seconds, then remove from the heat. Stir in the peanut butter.

4  Stir in the stock, a little at a time. Add the remaining ingredients and mix together to make a thick, creamy dressing.

5  Divide the vegetables between four plates and arrange the eggs on top. Drizzle the dressing over the salad and serve immediately.

✓ cows' milk-free   ✓ egg-free   ✓ gluten-free   ✓ wheat-free   ✓ nut-free   ✓ vegetarian   ✓ vegan   ✓ seafood-free

# Italian Baked Tomatoes with Curly Endive & Radicchio

## Nutritional details

### per 100 g

| | |
|---|---|
| energy | 68 kcals/284 kj |
| protein | 3 g |
| carbohydrate | 7 g |
| fat | 4 g |
| fibre | trace |
| sugar | trace |
| sodium | 0.3 g |

## Ingredients     Serves 4

1 tsp olive oil
4 beef tomatoes
salt
50 g/2 oz fresh white
   breadcrumbs
1 tbsp freshly snipped chives
1 tbsp freshly chopped parsley
125 g/4 oz button mushrooms,
   finely chopped
salt and freshly ground
   black pepper
25 g/1 oz fresh Parmesan
   cheese, grated

**For the salad:**
½ curly endive lettuce
½ small piece of radicchio
2 tbsp olive oil
1 tsp balsamic vinegar
salt and freshly ground
   black pepper

## Step-by-step guide

1  Preheat the oven to 190°C/ 375°F/Gas Mark 5. Lightly oil a baking tray with the teaspoon of oil. Slice the tops off the tomatoes and remove all the tomato flesh and sieve into a large bowl. Sprinkle a little salt inside the tomato shells and then place them upside down on a plate while the filling is prepared.

2  Mix the sieved tomato with the breadcrumbs, fresh herbs and mushrooms and season well with salt and pepper. Place the tomato shells on the prepared baking tray and fill with the tomato and mushroom mixture. Sprinkle the cheese on the top and bake in the preheated oven for 15–20 minutes, until golden brown.

3  Meanwhile, prepare the salad. Arrange the endive and radicchio on individual serving plates and mix the remaining ingredients together in a small bowl to make the dressing. Season to taste.

4  When the tomatoes are cooked, allow to rest for 5 minutes, then place on the prepared plates and drizzle over a little dressing. Serve warm.

# Lamb Meatballs with Savoy Cabbage

## Nutritional details

### per 100 g

| | |
|---|---|
| energy | 105 kcals/437 kj |
| protein | 8 g |
| carbohydrate | 5 g |
| fat | 6 g |
| fibre | trace |
| sugar | 0.4 g |
| sodium | 0.3 g |

## Ingredients          Serves 4

450 g/1 lb fresh lamb mince
1 tbsp freshly chopped parsley
1 tbsp freshly grated root ginger
1 tbsp light soy sauce
1 medium egg yolk
4 tbsp dark soy sauce
2 tbsp dry sherry
1 tbsp cornflour
3 tbsp vegetable oil
2 garlic cloves, peeled and chopped
1 bunch spring onions,
     trimmed and shredded
½ Savoy cabbage,
     trimmed and shredded
½ head Chinese leaves,
     trimmed and shredded
freshly chopped red chilli,
     to garnish

## Step-by-step guide

1  Place the lamb mince in a large bowl with the parsley, ginger, light soy sauce and egg yolk and mix together. Divide the mixture into walnut-sized pieces and, using your hands, roll into balls. Place on a baking sheet, cover with clingfilm and chill in the refrigerator for at least 30 minutes.

2  Meanwhile, blend together the dark soy sauce, sherry and cornflour with 2 tablespoons of water in a small bowl until smooth. Reserve.

3  Heat a wok, add the oil and when hot, add the meatballs and cook for 5–8 minutes, or until browned all over, turning occasionally. Using a slotted spoon, transfer the meatballs to a large plate and keep warm.

4  Add the garlic, spring onions, Savoy cabbage and the Chinese leaves to the wok and stir-fry for 3 minutes. Pour over the reserved soy sauce mixture, bring to the boil, then simmer for 30 seconds or until thickened. Return the meatballs to the wok and mix in. Garnish with chopped red chilli and serve immediately.

cows' milk-free   egg-free   gluten-free   wheat-free   nut-free   vegetarian   vegan   seafood-free

# Mushroom & Red Wine Pâté

## Nutritional details

### per 100 g

| | |
|---|---|
| energy | 72 kcals/303 kj |
| protein | 3 g |
| carbohydrate | 9 g |
| fat | 2 g |
| fibre | 1.1 g |
| sugar | 1.4 g |
| sodium | 0.1 g |

## Ingredients     Serves 4

3 large slices of white bread, crusts removed
2 tsp oil
1 small onion, peeled and finely chopped
1 garlic clove, peeled and crushed
350 g/12 oz button mushrooms, wiped and finely chopped
150 ml/¼ pint red wine
½ tsp dried mixed herbs
1 tbsp freshly chopped parsley
salt and freshly ground black pepper
2 tbsp low-fat cream cheese

**To serve:**
finely chopped cucumber
finely chopped tomato

## Step-by-step guide

1  Preheat the oven to 180°C/350°F/Gas Mark 4. Cut the bread in half diagonally. Place the bread triangles on a baking tray and cook for 10 minutes.

2  Remove from the oven and split each bread triangle in half to make 12 triangles and return to the oven until golden and crisp. Leave to cool on a wire rack.

3  Heat the oil in a saucepan and gently cook the onion and garlic until transparent.

4  Add the mushrooms and cook, stirring for 3–4 minutes or until the mushroom juices start to run.

5  Stir the wine and herbs into the mushroom mixture and bring to the boil. Reduce the heat and simmer uncovered until all the liquid is absorbed.

6  Remove from the heat and season to taste with salt and pepper. Leave to cool.

7  When cold, beat in the soft cream cheese and adjust the seasoning. Place in a small clean bowl and chill until required. Serve the toast triangles with the cucumber and tomato.

cows' milk-free   egg-free   gluten-free   wheat-free   nut-free   vegetarian   vegan   seafood-free

# Mushroom & Sherry Soup

## Nutritional details

### per 100 g

| | |
|---|---|
| energy | 98 kcals/412 kj |
| protein | 4 g |
| carbohydrate | 17 g |
| fat | 2 g |
| fibre | 0.8 g |
| sugar | 1.4 g |
| sodium | 0.4 g |

## Ingredients     Serves 4

4 slices day old white bread
zest of ½ lemon
1 tbsp lemon juice
salt and freshly ground
   black pepper
125 g/4 oz assorted wild
   mushrooms, lightly rinsed
125 g/4 oz baby button
   mushrooms, wiped
2 tsp olive oil
1 garlic clove, peeled
   and crushed
6 spring onions, trimmed
   and diagonally sliced
600 ml/1 pint vegetable stock
4 tbsp dry sherry
1 tbsp freshly snipped chives,
   to garnish

## Step-by-step guide

1 Preheat the oven to 180°C/350°F/ Gas Mark 4. Remove the crusts from the bread and cut the bread into small cubes.

2 In a large bowl toss the cubes of bread with the lemon rind and juice, 2 tablespoons of water and plenty of freshly ground black pepper.

3 Spread the bread cubes on to a lightly oiled, large baking tray and bake for 20 minutes until golden and crisp.

4 If the wild mushrooms are small, leave some whole. Otherwise, thinly slice all the mushrooms and reserve.

5 Heat the oil in a saucepan. Add the garlic and spring onions and cook for 1–2 minutes.

6 Add the mushrooms and cook for 3–4 minutes until they start to soften. Add the chicken stock and stir to mix.

7 Bring to the boil, then reduce the heat to a gentle simmer. Cover and cook for 10 minutes.

8 Stir in the sherry, and season to taste with a little salt and pepper. Pour into warmed bowls, sprinkle over the chives, and serve immediately with the lemon croûtons.

✓ cows' milk-free ✓ egg-free ✓ gluten-free ✓ wheat-free ✓ nut-free ✓ vegetarian ✓ vegan ✓ seafood-free

# Pasta Shells with Broccoli & Capers

## Nutritional details

### per 100 g

| | |
|---|---|
| energy | 136 kcals/569 kj |
| protein | 6 g |
| carbohydrate | 12 g |
| fat | 7 g |
| fibre | 1.7 g |
| sugar | 1.6 g |
| sodium | 0.2 g |

## Ingredients          Serves 4

400 g/14 oz conchiglie (shells)
450 g/1 lb broccoli florets, cut into
    small pieces
5 tbsp olive oil
1 large onion, peeled and
    finely chopped
4 tbsp capers in brine,
    rinsed and drained
½ tsp dried chilli flakes (optional)
75 g/3 oz freshly grated
    Parmesan cheese, plus
    extra to serve
25 g/1 oz pecorino cheese, grated
salt and freshly ground black pepper
2 tbsp freshly chopped flat leaf
    parsley, to garnish

## Step-by-step guide

1  Bring a large pan of lightly salted
   water to a rolling boil. Add the
   pasta shells, return to the boil
   and cook for 2 minutes. Add
   the broccoli to the pan. Return
   to the boil and continue cooking
   for 8–10 minutes, or until the
   conchiglie is 'al dente'.

2  Meanwhile, heat the olive oil in
   a large frying pan, add the onion
   and cook for 5 minutes, or until
   softened, stirring frequently. Stir in
   the capers and chilli flakes, if using,
   and cook for a further 2 minutes.

3  Drain the pasta and broccoli and
   add to the frying pan. Toss the
   ingredients to mix thoroughly.
   Sprinkle over the cheeses, then stir
   until the cheeses have just melted.
   Season to taste with salt and
   pepper, then tip into a warmed
   serving dish. Garnish with chopped
   parsley and serve immediately with
   extra Parmesan cheese.

cows' milk-free    egg-free    gluten-free    wheat-free    nut-free    vegetarian    vegan    seafood-free

# Pasta with Walnut Sauce

## Nutritional details

### per 100 g

| | |
|---|---|
| energy | 155 kcals/646 kj |
| protein | 5 g |
| carbohydrate | 13 g |
| fat | 10 g |
| fibre | 2 g |
| sugar | 0.9 g |
| sodium | trace |

## Ingredients     Serves 4

50 g/2 oz walnuts, toasted

3 spring onions, trimmed and chopped

2 garlic cloves, peeled and sliced

1 tbsp freshly chopped parsley or basil

5 tbsp extra virgin olive oil

salt and freshly ground black pepper

450 g/1 lb broccoli, cut into florets

350 g/12 oz pasta shapes

1 red chilli, deseeded and finely chopped

## Step-by-step guide

1  Place the toasted walnuts in a blender or food processor with the chopped spring onions, one of the garlic cloves and the parsley or basil. Blend to a fairly smooth paste, then gradually add 3 tablespoons of the olive oil until it is well mixed into the paste. Season the walnut paste to taste with salt and pepper and reserve.

2  Bring a large pan of lightly salted water to a rolling boil. Add the broccoli, return to the boil and cook for 2 minutes. Remove the broccoli, using a slotted draining spoon and refresh under cold running water. Drain again and pat dry on absorbent kitchen paper.

3  Bring the water back to a rolling boil. Add the pasta and cook according to the packet instructions, or until 'al dente'.

4  Meanwhile, heat the remaining oil in a frying pan. Add the remaining garlic and chilli. Cook gently for 2 minutes, or until softened. Add the broccoli and walnut paste. Cook for a further 3–4 minutes, or until heated through.

5  Drain the pasta thoroughly and transfer to a large, warmed serving bowl. Pour over the walnut and broccoli sauce. Toss together, adjust the seasoning and serve immediately.

cows' milk-free  egg-free  gluten-free  wheat-free  nut-free  vegetarian  vegan  seafood-free

# Rice & Papaya Salad

## Nutritional details

### per 100 g

| | |
|---|---|
| energy | 108 kcals/455 kj |
| protein | 8 g |
| carbohydrate | 17 g |
| fat | 2 g |
| fibre | 0.4 g |
| sugar | 1.7 g |
| sodium | trace |

## Ingredients          Serves 4

175 g/6 oz easy-cook basmati rice
1 cinnamon stick, bruised
1 bird's-eye chilli, deseeded
    and finely chopped
rind and juice of 2 limes
rind and juice of 2 lemons
2 tbsp Thai fish sauce
1 tbsp soft light brown sugar
1 papaya, peeled and seeds removed
1 mango, peeled and stone removed
1 green chilli, deseeded and
    finely chopped
2 tbsp freshly chopped coriander
1 tbsp freshly chopped mint
250 g/9 oz cooked chicken
50 g/2 oz roasted peanuts, chopped
strips of pitta bread, to serve

## Step-by-step guide

1   Rinse and drain the rice and pour into a saucepan. Add 450 ml/¾ pint boiling salted water and the cinnamon stick. Bring to the boil, reduce to a very low heat, then cover and cook without stirring for 15–18 minutes, or until all the liquid is absorbed. The rice should be light and fluffy and have steam holes on the surface. Remove the cinnamon stick and stir in the rind from 1 lime.

2   To make the dressing, place the bird's-eye chilli, remaining rind and lime and lemon juice, fish sauce and sugar in a food processor and mix until blended. Alternatively, place all the ingredients in a screw-top jar and shake until mixed. Pour half the dressing over the hot rice and toss until the rice glistens.

3   Slice the papaya and mango into thin slices, then place in a bowl. Add the chopped green chilli, coriander and mint. Place the chicken on a chopping board, then remove and discard any skin or sinews. Cut into fine shreds and add to the bowl with the chopped peanuts.

4   Add the remaining dressing to the chicken mixture and stir until all the ingredients are lightly coated. Spoon the rice onto a platter, pile the chicken mixture on top and serve with warm strips of pitta bread.

cows' milk-free   egg-free   gluten-free   wheat-free   nut-free   vegetarian   vegan   seafood-free

# Spinach Dumplings with Rich Tomato Sauce

## Nutritional details

### per 100 g

| | |
|---|---|
| energy | 107 kcals/447 kj |
| protein | 4 g |
| carbohydrate | 12 g |
| fat | 5 g |
| fibre | 1.1 g |
| sugar | 1.2 g |
| sodium | 0.2 g |

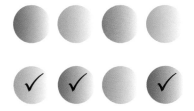
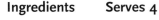

## Ingredients Serves 4

**For the sauce:**

2 tbsp olive oil
1 onion, peeled and chopped
1 garlic clove, peeled and crushed
1 red chilli, deseeded and chopped
150 ml/¼ pint dry white wine
400 g can chopped tomatoes
pared strip of lemon rind

**For the dumplings:**

450 g/1 lb fresh spinach
50 g/2 oz ricotta cheese
25 g/1 oz fresh white breadcrumbs
25 g/1 oz Parmesan cheese, grated
1 medium egg yolk
¼ tsp freshly grated nutmeg
salt and freshly ground black pepper
5 tbsp plain flour
2 tbsp olive oil, for frying
fresh basil leaves, to garnish
freshly cooked tagliatelle, to serve

## Step-by-step guide

1  To make the tomato sauce, heat the olive oil in a large saucepan and fry the onion gently for 5 minutes. Add the garlic and chilli and cook for a further 5 minutes, until softened.

2  Stir in the wine, chopped tomatoes and lemon rind. Bring to the boil, cover and simmer for 20 minutes, then uncover and simmer for 15 minutes, or until the sauce has thickened. Remove the lemon rind and season to taste with salt and pepper.

3  To make the spinach dumplings, wash the spinach thoroughly and remove any tough stalks. Cover and cook in a large saucepan over a low heat with just the water clinging to the leaves. Drain, then squeeze out all the excess water. Finely chop and put in a large bowl.

4  Add the ricotta, breadcrumbs, cheese and egg yolk to the spinach. Season with nutmeg and salt and pepper. Mix together and shape into 20 walnut-sized balls.

5  Toss the spinach balls in the flour. Heat the olive oil in a large, non-stick frying pan and fry the balls gently for 5–6 minutes, carefully turning occasionally. Garnish with fresh basil leaves and serve immediately with the tomato sauce and tagliatelle.

✓ cows' milk-free  ✓ egg-free  ✓ gluten-free  ✓ wheat-free  ✓ nut-free  ✓ vegetarian  ✓ vegan  ✓ seafood-free

# Stir-fried Greens

## Nutritional details

### per 100 g

| | |
|---|---|
| energy | 38 kcals/158 kj |
| protein | 2 g |
| carbohydrate | 5 g |
| fat | 2 g |
| fibre | trace |
| sugar | 1 g |
| sodium | 0.2 g |

## Ingredients    Serves 4

450 g/1 lb Chinese leaves
225 g/8 oz pak choi
225 g/8 oz broccoli florets
1 tbsp sesame seeds
1 tbsp groundnut oil
1 tbsp fresh root ginger,
    peeled and finely chopped
3 garlic cloves, peeled
    and finely chopped
2 red chillies, deseeded
    and split in half
50 ml/2 fl oz vegetable stock
2 tbsp Chinese rice wine
1 tbsp dark soy sauce
1 tsp light soy sauce
2 tsp black bean sauce
freshly ground black pepper
2 tsp sugar
1 tsp sesame oil

## Step-by-step guide

1  Separate the Chinese leaves and pak choi and wash well. Cut into 2.5 cm/1 inch strips. Separate the broccoli into small florets. Heat a wok or large frying pan, add the sesame seeds and stir-fry for 30 seconds or until browned.

2  Add the oil to the wok and when hot, add the ginger, garlic and chillies and stir-fry for 30 seconds. Add the broccoli and stir-fry for 1 minute. Add the Chinese leaves and pak choi and stir-fry for a further 1 minute.

3  Pour the vegetable stock and Chinese rice wine into the wok with the soy and black bean sauces. Season to taste with pepper and add the sugar. Reduce the heat and simmer for 6–8 minutes, or until the vegetables are tender but still firm to the bite. Tip into a warmed serving dish, removing the chillies if preferred. Drizzle with the sesame oil and serve immediately.

✓ cows' milk-free  ✓ egg-free  ✓ gluten-free  ✓ wheat-free  ✓ nut-free  ✓ vegetarian  ✓ vegan  ✓ seafood-free

# Sweet Potato Crisps with Mango Salsa

## Nutritional details

### per 100 g

| | |
|---|---|
| energy | 100 kcals/419 kj |
| protein | 2 g |
| carbohydrate | 17 g |
| fat | 4 g |
| fibre | 1.3 g |
| sugar | 6.5 g |
| sodium | 0.2 |

**For the salsa:**

1 large mango, peeled, stoned and cut into small cubes
8 cherry tomatoes, quartered
½ cucumber, peeled if preferred and finely diced
1 red onion, peeled and finely chopped
pinch of sugar
1 red chilli, deseeded and finely chopped
2 tbsp rice vinegar
2 tbsp olive oil
grated rind and juice of 1 lime

450 g/1 lb sweet potatoes, peeled and thinly sliced
vegetable oil, for deep frying
sea salt
2 tbsp freshly chopped mint

## Step-by-step guide

1 To make the salsa, mix the mango with the tomatoes, cucumber and onion. Add the sugar, chilli, vinegar, oil and the lime rind and juice. Mix together thoroughly, cover and leave for 45–50 minutes.

2 Soak the potatoes in cold water for 40 minutes to remove as much of the excess starch as possible. Drain and dry thoroughly in a clean tea towel, or absorbent kitchen paper.

3 Heat the oil to 190°C/375°F in a deep fryer. When at the correct temperature, place half the potatoes in the frying basket, then carefully lower the potatoes into the hot oil and cook for 4–5 minutes, or until they are golden brown, shaking the basket every minute so that they do not stick together.

4 Drain the potato crisps on absorbent kitchen paper, sprinkle with sea salt and place under a preheated moderate grill for a few seconds to dry out. Repeat with the remaining potatoes. Stir the mint into the salsa and serve with the potato crisps.

✓ cows' milk-free  ✓ egg-free  ✓ gluten-free  ✓ wheat-free  ✓ nut-free  ✓ vegetarian  ✓ vegan  ✓ seafood-free

# Tagliatelle with Broccoli & Sesame

## Nutritional details

### per 100 g

| | |
|---|---|
| energy | 104 kcals/440 kj |
| protein | 5 g |
| carbohydrate | 15 g |
| fat | 4 g |
| fibre | 1.9 g |
| sugar | 4.7 g |
| sodium | 0.5 g |

## Ingredients    Serves 2

225 g/8 oz broccoli,
   cut into florets
125 g/4 oz baby corn
175 g/6 oz dried tagliatelle
1½ tbsp tahini paste
1 tbsp dark soy sauce
1 tbsp dark muscovado sugar
1 tbsp red wine vinegar
1 tbsp sunflower oil
1 garlic clove, peeled
   and finely chopped
2.5 cm/1 inch piece fresh
   root ginger, peeled
   and shredded
½ tsp dried chilli flakes
salt and freshly ground
   black pepper
1 tbsp toasted sesame seeds
slices of radish,
   to garnish

## Step-by-step guide

1 Bring a large saucepan of salted water to the boil and add the broccoli and corn. Return the water to the boil then remove the vegetables at once using a slotted spoon, reserving the water. Plunge them into cold water and drain well. Dry on kitchen paper and reserve.

2 Return the water to the boil. Add the tagliatelle and cook until 'al dente' or according to the packet instructions. Drain well. Run under cold water until cold, then drain well again.

3 Place the tahini, soy sauce, sugar and vinegar into a bowl. Mix well, then reserve. Heat the oil in a wok or large frying pan over a high heat and add the garlic, ginger and chilli flakes and stir-fry for about 30 seconds. Add the broccoli and baby corn and continue to stir-fry for about 3 minutes.

4 Add the tagliatelle to the wok along with the tahini mixture and stir together for a further 1–2 minutes until heated through. Season to taste with salt and pepper. Sprinkle with sesame seeds, garnish with the radish slices and serve immediately.

cows' milk-free · egg-free · gluten-free · wheat-free · nut-free · vegetarian · vegan · seafood-free

# Teriyaki Turkey with Oriental Vegetables

## Nutritional details

### per 100 g

| | |
|---|---|
| energy | 79 kcals/335 kj |
| protein | 9 g |
| carbohydrate | 7 g |
| fat | 2 g |
| fibre | 1 g |
| sugar | 1.5 g |
| sodium | 0.2 g |

## Ingredients        Serves 4

1 red chilli
1 garlic clove, peeled
    and crushed
2.5 cm/1 inch piece root ginger,
    peeled and grated
3 tbsp dark soy sauce
1 tsp sunflower oil
350 g/12 oz skinless,
    boneless turkey breast
1 tbsp sesame oil
1 tbsp sesame seeds
2 carrots, peeled and cut into
    matchstick strips
1 leek, trimmed and shredded
125 g/4 oz broccoli,
    cut into tiny florets
1 tsp cornflour
3 tbsp dry sherry
125 g/4 oz mangetout,
    cut into thin strips

### To serve:
freshly cooked egg noodles
sprinkling of sesame seeds

## Step-by-step guide

1   Halve, deseed and thinly slice the chilli. Put into a small bowl with the garlic, ginger, soy sauce and sunflower oil.

2   Cut the turkey into thin strips. Add to the mixture and mix until well coated. Cover with clingfilm and marinate in the refrigerator for at least 30 minutes.

3   Heat a wok or large frying pan. Add 2 teaspoons of the sesame oil. When hot, remove the turkey from the marinade. Stir-fry for 2–3 minutes until browned and cooked. Remove from the pan and reserve.

4   Heat the remaining 1 teaspoon of oil in the wok. Add the sesame seeds and stir-fry for a few seconds until they start to change colour.

5   Add the carrots, leek and broccoli and continue stir-frying for 2–3 minutes.

6   Blend the cornflour with 1 tablespoon of cold water to make a smooth paste. Stir in the sherry and marinade. Add to the wok with the mangetout and cook for 1 minute, stirring all the time until thickened.

7   Return the turkey to the pan and continue cooking for 1–2 minutes or until the turkey is hot, the vegetables are tender and the sauce is bubbling. Serve the turkey and vegetables immediately with the egg noodles. Sprinkle with the sesame seeds.

cows' milk-free  ✓ egg-free  ✓ gluten-free  ✓ wheat-free  ✓ nut-free  vegetarian  ✓ vegan  seafood-free

# Thai Noodles & Vegetables with Tofu

## Nutritional details

### per 100 g

| | |
|---|---|
| energy | 52 kcals/217 kj |
| protein | 4 g |
| carbohydrate | 7 g |
| fat | 1 g |
| fibre | 0.4 g |
| sugar | 0.7 g |
| sodium | 0.5 g |

## Ingredients    Serves 4

225 g/8 oz firm tofu
2 tbsp soy sauce
rind of 1 lime, grated
2 lemon grass stalks
1 red chilli
1 litre/1¾ pint vegetable stock
2 slices fresh root
    ginger, peeled
2 garlic cloves, peeled
2 sprigs of fresh coriander
175 g/6 oz dried thread
    egg noodles
125 g/4 oz shiitake or button
    mushrooms, sliced if large
2 carrots, peeled and
    cut into matchsticks
125 g/4 oz mangetout
125 g/4 oz pak choi or
    other Chinese leaf
1 tbsp freshly
    chopped coriander
salt and freshly ground
    black pepper
coriander sprigs, to garnish

## Step-by-step guide

1  Drain the tofu well and cut into cubes. Put into a shallow dish with the soy sauce and lime rind. Stir well to coat and leave to marinate for 30 minutes.

2  Meanwhile, put the lemon grass and chilli on a chopping board and bruise with the side of a large knife, ensuring the blade is pointing away from you. Put the vegetable stock in a large saucepan and add the lemon grass, chilli, ginger, garlic, and coriander. Bring to the boil, cover and simmer gently for 20 minutes.

3  Strain the stock into a clean pan. Return to the boil and add the noodles, tofu and its marinade and the mushrooms. Simmer gently for 4 minutes.

4  Add the carrots, mangetout, pak choi and coriander and simmer for a further 3–4 minutes until the vegetables are just tender. Season to taste with salt and pepper. Garnish with coriander sprigs and serve immediately.

cows' milk-free   egg-free   gluten-free   wheat-free   nut-free   vegetarian   vegan   seafood-free

33

# Tomato & Basil Soup

## Nutritional details

### per 100 g

| | |
|---|---|
| energy | 41 kcals/171 kj |
| protein | 2 g |
| carbohydrate | 8 g |
| fat | 1 g |
| fibre | trace |
| sugar | 2.8 g |
| sodium | 0.1 g |

## Ingredients          Serves 4

1.1 kg/ 2½ lb ripe
   tomatoes, cut in half
2 garlic cloves
1 tsp olive oil
1 tbsp balsamic vinegar
1 tbsp dark brown sugar
1 tbsp tomato purée
300 ml/½ pint vegetable stock
6 tbsp low-fat natural yogurt
2 tbsp freshly chopped basil
salt and freshly ground
   black pepper
small basil leaves,
   to garnish

## Step-by-step guide

1  Preheat the oven to 200°C/ 400°F/ Gas Mark 6. Evenly spread the tomatoes and unpeeled garlic in a single layer in a large roasting tin.

2  Mix the oil and vinegar together. Drizzle over the tomatoes and sprinkle with the dark brown sugar.

3  Roast the tomatoes in the preheated oven for 20 minutes until tender and lightly charred in places.

4  Remove from the oven and allow to cool slightly. When cool enough to handle, squeeze the softened flesh of the garlic from the papery skin. Place with the charred tomatoes in a nylon sieve over a saucepan.

5  Press the garlic and tomato through the sieve with the back of a wooden spoon.

6  When all the flesh has been sieved, add the tomato purée and vegetable stock to the pan. Heat gently, stirring occasionally.

7  In a small bowl beat the yogurt and basil together and season to taste with salt and pepper. Stir the basil yogurt into the soup. Garnish with basil leaves and serve immediately.

☑ cows' milk-free   ☑ egg-free   ☑ gluten-free   ☑ wheat-free   ☑ nut-free   ☑ vegetarian   ☑ vegan   ☑ seafood-free

# Vegetable Biryani

## Nutritional details

### per 100 g

| | |
|---|---|
| energy | 94 kcals/393 kj |
| protein | 2 g |
| carbohydrate | 18 g |
| fat | 2 g |
| fibre | 0.9 g |
| sugar | 4 g |
| sodium | 0.1 g |

## Ingredients    Serves 4

2 tbsp vegetable oil, plus a little
     extra for brushing
2 large onions, peeled and thinly
     sliced lengthwise
2 garlic cloves, peeled and
     finely chopped
2.5 cm/1 inch piece fresh root ginger,
     peeled and finely grated
1 small carrot, peeled and
     cut into sticks
1 small parsnip, peeled and diced
1 small sweet potato chunks,
     peeled and diced
1 tbsp medium curry paste
225 g/8 oz basmati rice
4 ripe tomatoes, peeled,
     deseeded and diced
600 ml/1 pint vegetable stock
175 g/6 oz cauliflower florets
50 g/2 oz peas, thawed if frozen
salt and freshly ground black pepper

**To garnish:**
roasted cashew nuts
raisins
fresh coriander leaves

### Step-by-step guide

1   Preheat the oven to 200°C/400°F/ Gas Mark 6. Put 1 tablespoon of the vegetable oil in a large bowl with the onions and toss to coat. Lightly brush or spray a non-stick baking sheet with a little more oil. Spread half the onions on the baking sheet and cook at the top of the preheated oven for 25–30 minutes, stirring regularly, until golden and crisp. Remove from the oven and reserve for the garnish.

2   Meanwhile, heat a large flameproof casserole dish over a medium heat and add the remaining oil and onions. Cook for 5–7 minutes until softened and starting to brown. Add a little water if they start to stick. Add the garlic and ginger and cook for another minute, then add the carrot, parsnip and sweet potato. Cook the vegetables for a further 5 minutes. Add the curry paste and stir for a minute until everything is coated, then stir in the rice and tomatoes. After 2 minutes add the stock and stir well. Bring to the boil, cover and simmer over a very gentle heat for about 10 minutes.

3   Add the cauliflower and peas and cook for 8–10 minutes, or until the rice is tender. Season to taste with salt and pepper. Serve garnished with the crispy onions, cashew nuts, raisins and coriander.

# Vegetables Braised in Olive Oil & Lemon

## Nutritional details

### per 100 g

| | |
|---|---|
| energy | 72 kcals/297 kj |
| protein | 2 g |
| carbohydrate | 2 g |
| fat | 6 g |
| fibre | 1.4 g |
| sugar | 1.1 g |
| sodium | trace |

## Ingredients     Serves 4

small strip of pared rind
   and juice of ½ lemon
4 tbsp olive oil
1 bay leaf
large sprig of thyme
150 ml/¼ pint water
4 spring onions, trimmed
   and finely chopped
175 g/6 oz baby button mushrooms
175 g/6 oz broccoli,
   cut into small florets
175 g/6 oz cauliflower,
   cut into small florets
1 medium courgette,
   sliced on the diagonal
2 tbsp freshly snipped chives
salt and freshly ground
   black pepper
lemon zest, to garnish

## Step-by-step guide

1 Put the pared lemon rind and juice into a large saucepan. Add the olive oil, bay leaf, thyme and the water. Bring to the boil. Add the spring onions and mushrooms. Top with the broccoli and cauliflower, trying to add them so that the stalks are submerged in the water and the tops are just above it. Cover and simmer for 3 minutes.

2 Scatter the courgettes on top, so that they are steamed rather than boiled. Cook, covered, for a further 3–4 minutes, until all the vegetables are tender. Using a slotted spoon, transfer the vegetables from the liquid into a warmed serving dish. Increase the heat and boil rapidly for 3–4 minutes, or until the liquid is reduced to about 8 tablespoons. Remove the lemon rind, bay leaf and thyme sprig and discard.

3 Stir the chives into the reduced liquid, season to taste with salt and pepper and pour over the vegetables. Sprinkle with lemon zest and serve immediately.

✓ cows' milk-free  ✓ egg-free  ✓ gluten-free  ✓ wheat-free  ✓ nut-free  ✓ vegetarian  ✓ vegan  ✓ seafood-free

# Wild Garlic Mushrooms with Pizza Breadsticks

## Nutritional details

### per 100 g

| | |
|---|---|
| energy | 249 kcals/1045 kj |
| protein | 6 g |
| carbohydrate | 32 g |
| fat | 12 g |
| fibre | 1.3 g |
| sugar | 0.6 g |
| sodium | 0.2 g |

## Ingredients    Serves 6

**For the breadsticks:**

7 g/¼ oz dried yeast
250 ml/8 fl oz warm water
400 g/14 oz strong, plain flour
2 tbsp olive oil
1 tsp salt

**For the mushrooms:**

9 tbsp olive oil
4 garlic cloves, peeled
    and crushed
450 g/1 lb mixed wild
    mushrooms, wiped
    and dried
salt and freshly ground
    black pepper
1 tbsp freshly chopped parsley
1 tbsp freshly chopped basil
1 tsp fresh oregano leaves
juice of 1 lemon

## Step-by-step guide

1 Preheat the oven to 240°C/ 475°F/Gas Mark 9, 15 minutes before baking. Place the dried yeast in the warm water for 10 minutes. Place the flour in a large bowl and gradually blend in the olive oil, salt and the dissolved yeast.

2 Knead on a lightly floured surface to form a smooth and pliable dough. Cover with clingfilm and leave in a warm place for 15 minutes to allow the dough to rise, then roll out again and cut into sticks of equal length. Cover and leave to rise again for 10 minutes. Brush with the olive oil, sprinkle with salt and bake in the preheated oven for 10 minutes.

3 Pour 3 tablespoons of the oil into a frying pan and add the crushed garlic. Cook over a very low heat, stirring well for 3–4 minutes to flavour the oil.

4 Cut the wild mushrooms into bite-sized slices if very large, then add to the pan. Season well with salt and pepper and cook very gently for 6–8 minutes, or until tender.

5 Whisk the fresh herbs, the remaining olive oil and lemon juice together. Pour over the mushrooms and heat through. Season to taste and place on individual serving dishes. Serve with the pizza breadsticks.

cows' milk-free   egg-free   gluten-free   wheat-free   nut-free   vegetarian   vegan   seafood-free

# Wild Mushroom Risotto

## Nutritional details

### per 100 g

| | |
|---|---|
| energy | 113 kcals/471 kj |
| protein | 5 g |
| carbohydrate | 9 g |
| fat | 6 g |
| fibre | 0.2 g |
| sugar | 1.1 g |
| sodium | 0.5 g |

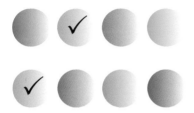

## Ingredients    Serves 4

15 g/½ oz dried porcini
1.1 litres/2 pints vegetable stock
75 g/3 oz butter
1 tbsp olive oil
1 onion, peeled and chopped
2–4 garlic cloves, peeled and chopped
1–2 red chillies, deseeded and chopped
225 g/8 oz wild mushrooms,
    wiped and halved, if large
125 g/4 oz button mushrooms,
    wiped and sliced
350 g/12 oz Arborio rice
175 g/6 oz large cooked
    prawns, peeled
150 ml/¼ pint white wine
salt and freshly ground black pepper
1 tbsp lemon zest
1 tbsp freshly snipped chives
2 tbsp freshly chopped parsley

## Step-by-step guide

1   Soak the porcini in 300 ml/
    ½ pint of very hot but not boiling
    water for 30 minutes. Drain,
    reserving the mushrooms and
    soaking liquid. Pour the stock
    into a saucepan, and bring to the
    boil, then reduce the heat to keep
    it simmering.

2   Melt the butter and oil in a
    large, deep frying pan, add the
    onion, garlic and chillies and
    cook gently for 5 minutes.
    Add the wild and button
    mushrooms with the drained
    porcini, and continue to cook for
    4–5 minutes, stirring frequently.

3   Stir in the rice and cook for
    1 minute. Strain the reserved
    soaking liquid and stir into the rice
    with a little of the hot stock. Cook
    gently, stirring frequently, until the
    liquid is absorbed. Continue to
    add most of the stock, a ladleful
    at a time, cooking after each
    addition, until the rice is tender
    and the risotto looks creamy.

4   Add the prawns and wine along
    with the last additions of stock.
    When the prawns are hot and
    all the liquid is absorbed, season
    to taste with salt and pepper.
    Remove from the heat and stir
    in the lemon zest, chives and
    parsley, reserving some for the
    garnish. Garnish and serve.

✓ cows' milk-free   ✓ egg-free   ✓ gluten-free   ✓ wheat-free   ✓ nut-free   vegetarian   ✓ vegan   seafood-free

# Autumn Fruit Layer

## Nutritional details

### per 100 g

| | |
|---|---|
| energy | 198 kcals/828 kj |
| protein | 4 g |
| carbohydrate | 27 g |
| fat | 9 g |
| fibre | 1.8 g |
| sugar | 15.6 g |
| sodium | 0.2 g |

## Ingredients     Serves 4

450 g/1 lb Bramley
    cooking apples
225 g/8 oz blackberries
50 g/2 oz soft brown sugar
juice of 1 lemon
50 g/2 oz low-fat spread
200 g/7 oz breadcrumbs
225 g/8 oz honey-coated nut
    mix, chopped
redcurrants and mint leaves,
    to decorate
half-fat whipped cream
    or reduced-fat ice
    cream, to serve

## Step-by-step guide

1  Peel, core and slice the cooking apples and place in a saucepan with the blackberries, sugar and lemon juice.

2  Cover the fruit mixture and simmer, stirring occasionally for about 15 minutes or until the apples and blackberries have formed a thick purée.

3  Remove the pan from the heat and allow to cool.

4  Melt the low-fat spread in a frying pan and cook the breadcrumbs for 5–10 minutes, stirring occasionally until golden and crisp.

5  Remove the pan from the heat and stir in the nuts. Allow to cool.

6  Alternately layer the fruit purée and breadcrumbs into four tall glasses.

7  Store the desserts in the refrigerator to chill and remove when ready to serve.

8  Decorate with redcurrants and mint leaves and serve with half-fat whipped cream or a reduced-fat vanilla or raspberry ice cream.

cows' milk-free   ✓ egg-free   ✓ gluten-free   ✓ wheat-free   ✓ nut-free   ✓ vegetarian   ✓ vegan   ✓ seafood-free

# Caramelised Oranges in an Iced Bowl

## Nutritional details

### per 100 g

| | |
|---|---|
| energy | 91 kcals/388 kj |
| protein | 1 g |
| carbohydrate | 23 g |
| fat | trace |
| fibre | 1.4 g |
| sugar | 23 g |
| sodium | trace |

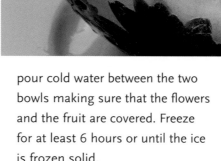

## Ingredients          Serves 4

**For the ice bowl:**
about 36 ice cubes
fresh flowers and fruits
8 medium-sized oranges
225 g/8 oz caster sugar
4 tbsp Grand Marnier
    or Cointreau

## Step-by-step guide

1  Set the freezer to rapid freeze. Place a few ice cubes in the base of a 1.7 litre/3 pint freezable glass bowl. Place a 900 ml/1½ pint glass bowl on top of the ice cubes. Arrange the flower heads and fruits in between the two bowls, wedging into position with the ice cubes.

2  Weigh down the smaller bowl with some heavy weights, then carefully pour cold water between the two bowls making sure that the flowers and the fruit are covered. Freeze for at least 6 hours or until the ice is frozen solid.

3  When ready to use, remove the weights and, using a hot damp cloth, rub the inside of the smaller bowl with the cloth until it loosens sufficiently for you to remove the bowl. Place the larger bowl in the sink or washing-up bowl, half filled with very hot water. Leave for about 30 seconds or until the ice loosens. Take care not to leave the bowl in the water for too long otherwise the ice will melt. Remove the bowl and leave in the refrigerator. Return the freezer to its normal setting.

4  Thinly pare the rind from 2 oranges and then cut into julienne strips. Using a sharp knife cut away the rind and pith from all the oranges, holding over a bowl to catch the juices. Slice the oranges, discarding any pips and reform each orange back to its original shape. Secure with cocktail sticks, then place in a bowl.

5  Heat 300 ml/½ pint water, orange rind and sugar together in a pan. Stir the sugar until dissolved. Bring to the boil. Boil for 15 minutes, until it is a caramel colour. Remove the pan from heat.

6  Stir in the liqueur, pour over the oranges. Allow to cool. Chill for 3 hours, turning the oranges occasionally. Spoon into the ice bowl and serve.

cows' milk-free    egg-free    gluten-free    wheat-free    nut-free    vegetarian    vegan    seafood-free

# Creamy Puddings with Mixed Berry Compote

## Nutritional details

### per 100 g

| | |
|---|---|
| energy | 232 kcals/968 kj |
| protein | 5 g |
| carbohydrate | 18 g |
| fat | 16 g |
| fibre | 0.4 g |
| sugar | 15 g |
| sodium | trace |

## Ingredients  Serves 6

300 ml/½ pint half-fat
    double cream
1 x 250 g carton
    ricotta cheese
50 g/2 oz caster sugar
125 g/4 oz white chocolate,
    broken into pieces
350 g/12 oz mixed summer
    fruits such as strawberries,
    blueberries and raspberries
2 tbsp Cointreau

## Step-by-step guide

1  Set the freezer to rapid freeze. Whip the cream until soft peaks form. Fold in the ricotta cheese and half the sugar.

2  Place the chocolate in a bowl set over a saucepan of simmering water. Stir until melted.

3  Remove from the heat and leave to cool, stirring occasionally. Stir into the cheese mixture until well blended.

4  Spoon the mixture into six individual pudding moulds and level the surface of each pudding with the back of a spoon. Place in the freezer and freeze for 4 hours.

5  Place the fruits and the remaining sugar in a pan and heat gently, stirring occasionally until the sugar has dissolved and the juices are just beginning to run. Stir in the Cointreau to taste.

6  Dip the pudding moulds in hot water for 30 seconds and invert on to six serving plates. Spoon the fruit compote over the puddings and serve immediately. Remember to return the freezer to its normal setting.

cows' milk-free  egg-free  gluten-free  wheat-free  nut-free  vegetarian  vegan  seafood-free

# Grape & Almond Layer

## Nutritional details

### per 100 g

| | |
|---|---|
| energy | 97 kcals/409 kj |
| protein | 3 g |
| carbohydrate | 18 g |
| fat | 2 g |
| fibre | 0.4 g |
| sugar | 10.7 g |
| sodium | trace |

## Ingredients    Serves 4

300 ml/½ pint low-fat
    fromage frais
300 ml/½ pint half-fat
    Greek-set yogurt
3 tbsp icing sugar, sifted
2 tbsp crème de cassis
450 g/1 lb red grapes
175 g/6 oz Amaretti biscuits
2 ripe passion fruit

**To decorate:**
icing sugar
extra grapes, optional

## Step-by-step guide

1  Mix together the fromage frais and yogurt in a bowl and lightly fold in the sifted icing sugar and crème de cassis with a large metal spoon or rubber spatula until lightly blended.

2  Using a small knife, remove the seeds from the grapes if necessary. Rinse lightly and pat dry on absorbent kitchen paper.

3  Place the deseeded grapes in a bowl and stir in any juice from the grapes from deseeding.

4  Place the Amaretti biscuits in a polythene bag and crush roughly with a rolling pin. Alternatively, use a food processor.

5  Cut the passion fruit in half, scoop out the seeds with a teaspoon and reserve.

6  Divide the yogurt mixture between four tall glasses, then layer alternately with grapes, crushed biscuits and most of the passion fruit seeds. Top with the yogurt mixture and the remaining passion fruit seeds. Chill for 1 hour and decorate with extra grapes. Lightly dust with icing sugar and serve.

✓ cows' milk-free  ✓ egg-free  ✓ gluten-free  ✓ wheat-free  ✓ nut-free  ✓ vegetarian  ✓ vegan  ✓ seafood-free

# Orange Freeze

## Nutritional details

### per 100 g

| | |
|---|---|
| energy | 72 kcals/303 kj |
| protein | 1 g |
| carbohydrate | 14 g |
| fat | 1 g |
| fibre | 1.5 g |
| sugar | 8.5 g |
| sodium | trace |

## Ingredients    Serves 4

4 large oranges
about 300 ml/½ pint low-fat
    vanilla ice cream
225 g/8 oz raspberries
75 g/3 oz icing sugar, sifted
redcurrant sprigs, to decorate

## Step-by-step guide

1  Set the freezer to rapid freeze. Using a sharp knife carefully cut the lid off each orange.

2  Scoop out the flesh from the orange, discarding any pips and thick pith.

3  Place the shells and lids in the freezer and chop any remaining orange flesh.

4  Whisk together the orange juice, orange flesh and vanilla ice cream, until well blended.

5  Cover and freeze, for about 2 hours, occasionally breaking up the ice crystals with a fork or a whisk. Stir the mixture from around the edge of the container into the centre, then level and return to the freezer. Do this 2–3 times then leave until almost frozen solid.

6  Place a large scoop of the ice cream mixture into the frozen shells. Add another scoop on top, so that there is plenty outside of the orange shell and return to the freezer for 1 hour.

7  Arrange the lids on top and freeze for a further 2 hours, until the filled orange shell is completely frozen solid.

8  Meanwhile, using a nylon sieve press the raspberries into a bowl using the back of a wooden spoon and mix together with the icing sugar. Spoon the raspberry coulis on to four serving plates and place an orange at the centre of each. Dust with icing sugar and serve decorated with the redcurrants. Remember to return the freezer to its normal setting.

cows' milk-free   egg-free   gluten-free   wheat-free   nut-free   vegetarian   vegan   seafood-free

# Raspberry Sorbet Crush

## Nutritional details

### per 100 g

| | |
|---|---|
| energy | 134 kcals/570 kj |
| protein | 1 g |
| carbohydrate | 34 g |
| fat | 0.2 g |
| fibre | 0.7 g |
| sugar | 29.9 g |
| sodium | trace |

## Ingredients          Serves 4

225 g/8 oz raspberries,
    thawed if frozen
grated rind and juice of 1 lime
300 ml/½ pint orange juice
225 g/8 oz caster sugar
2 medium egg whites

## Step-by-step guide

1   Set the freezer to rapid freeze. If using fresh raspberries, pick over and lightly rinse.

2   Place the raspberries in a dish and, using a potato masher, mash to a chunky purée.

3   Place the lime rind and juice, orange juice and half the caster sugar in a large, heavy-based saucepan.

4   Heat gently, stirring frequently until the sugar is dissolved. Bring to the boil and boil rapidly for about 5 minutes.

5   Remove the pan from the heat and pour carefully into a freezable container.

6   Leave to cool, then place in the freezer and freeze for 2 hours, stirring occasionally to break up the ice crystals.

7   Fold the ice mixture into the raspberry purée with a metal spoon and freeze for a further 2 hours, stirring occasionally.

8   Whisk the egg whites until stiff. Then gradually whisk in the remaining caster sugar a tablespoon at a time until the egg white mixture is stiff and glossy.

9   Fold into the raspberry sorbet with a metal spoon and freeze for 1 hour. Spoon into tall glasses and serve immediately. Remember to return the freezer to its normal setting.

cows' milk-free  ✓ egg-free  ✓ gluten-free  ✓ wheat-free  ✓ nut-free  ✓ vegetarian  ✓ vegan  ✓ seafood-free

# Raspberry Soufflé

## Nutritional details

### per 100 g

| | |
|---|---|
| energy | 79 kcals/333 kj |
| protein | 4 g |
| carbohydrate | 9 g |
| fat | 3 g |
| fibre | 1,5 g |
| sugar | 9.1 g |
| sodium | trace |

## Ingredients      Serves 4

125 g/4 oz redcurrants
50 g/2 oz caster sugar
1 sachet (3 tsp) powdered gelatine
3 medium eggs, separated
300 g/½ pint half-fat Greek yogurt
450 g/1 lb raspberries,
    thawed if frozen

**To decorate:**
mint sprigs
extra fruits

## Step-by-step guide

1 Wrap a band of double thickness greaseproof paper around four ramekin dishes, making sure that 5 cm/2 inches of the paper stays above the top of each dish. Secure the paper to the dish with an elastic band or Sellotape.

2 Place the redcurrants and 1 tablespoon of the sugar in a small saucepan. Cook for 5 minutes until softened. Remove from the heat, sieve and reserve.

3 Place 3 tablespoons of water in a small bowl and sprinkle over the gelatine. Allow to stand for 5 minutes until spongy. Place the bowl over a pan of simmering water and leave until dissolved. Remove and allow to cool.

4 Beat together the remaining sugar and egg yolks until pale thick and creamy, then fold in the yogurt with a metal spoon or rubber spatula until well blended.

5 Sieve the raspberries and fold into the yogurt mixture with the gelatine. Whisk the egg whites until stiff and fold into the yogurt mixture. Pour into the prepared dishes and chill in the refrigerator for 2 hours until firm.

6 Remove the paper from the dishes and spread the redcurrant purée over the top of the soufflés. Decorate with mint sprigs and extra fruits and serve.

# Summer Fruit Semifreddo

## Nutritional details

### per 100 g

| | |
|---|---|
| energy | 309 kcals/1277 kj |
| protein | 3 g |
| carbohydrate | 9 g |
| fat | 29 g |
| fibre | 0.6 g |
| sugar | 5 g |
| sodium | trace |

## Ingredients    Serves 6–8

225 g/8 oz raspberries
125 g/4 oz blueberries
125 g/4 oz redcurrants
50 g/2 oz icing sugar
juice of 1 lemon
1 vanilla pod, split
50 g/2 oz sugar
4 large eggs, separated
600 ml/1 pint double cream
pinch of salt
fresh redcurrants, to decorate

## Step-by-step guide

1   Wash and hull or remove stalks from the fruits, as necessary, then put them into a food processor or blender with the icing sugar and lemon juice. Blend to a purée, pour into a jug and chill in the refrigerator, until needed.

2   Remove the seeds from the vanilla pod by opening the pod and scraping with the back of a knife. Add the seeds to the sugar and whisk with the egg yolks until pale and thick.

3   In another bowl, whip the cream until soft peaks form. Do not overwhip. In a third bowl, whip the egg whites with the salt until stiff peaks form.

4   Using a large metal spoon – to avoid knocking any air from the mixture – fold together the fruit purée, egg yolk mixture, the cream and egg whites. Transfer the mixture to a round, shallow, lidded freezer box and put into the freezer until almost frozen. If the mixture freezes solid, thaw in the refrigerator until semi-frozen. Turn out the semi-frozen mixture, cut into wedges and serve decorated with a few fresh redcurrants. If the mixture thaws completely, eat immediately and do not refreeze.

cows' milk-free   egg-free   gluten-free   wheat-free   nut-free   vegetarian   vegan   seafood-free

# Summer Pavlova

## Nutritional details

### per 100 g

| | |
|---|---|
| energy | 123 kcals/520 kj |
| protein | 2 g |
| carbohydrate | 28 g |
| fat | 1 g |
| fibre | 0.8 g |
| sugar | 25 g |
| sodium | trace |

## Ingredients    Serves 6–8

4 medium egg whites
225 g/8 oz caster sugar
1 tsp vanilla essence
2 tsp white wine vinegar
1½ tsp cornflour
300 ml/½ pint half-fat
    Greek-set yogurt
2 tbsp honey
225 g/8 oz strawberries, hulled
125 g/4 oz raspberries
125 g/4 oz blueberries
4 kiwis, peeled and sliced
icing sugar, to decorate

## Step-by-step guide

1  Preheat the oven to 150°C/300°F/ Gas Mark 2. Line a baking sheet with a sheet of greaseproof or baking parchment.

2  Place the egg whites in a clean, grease-free bowl and whisk until very stiff.

3  Whisk in half the sugar, vanilla essence, vinegar and cornflour, continue whisking until stiff.

4  Gradually, whisk in the remaining sugar, a teaspoonful at a time until very stiff and glossy.

5  Using a large spoon, arrange spoonfuls of the meringue in a circle on the greaseproof paper or baking parchment paper.

6  Bake in the preheated oven for 1 hour until crisp and dry. Turn the oven off and leave the meringue in the oven to cool completely.

7  Remove the meringue from the baking sheet and peel away the parchment paper. Mix together the yogurt and honey. Place the pavlova on a serving plate and spoon the yogurt into the centre.

8  Scatter over the strawberries, raspberries, blueberries and kiwis. Dust with the icing sugar and serve.

# Summer Pudding

## Nutritional details

### per 100 g

| | |
|---|---|
| energy | 154 kcals/657 kj |
| protein | 3 g |
| carbohydrate | 36 g |
| fat | 0.7 g |
| fibre | 1.9 g |
| sugar | 20.2 g |
| sodium | 0.2 g |

## Ingredients    Serves 4

450 g/1 lb redcurrants
125 g/4 oz caster sugar
350 g/12 oz strawberries,
  hulled and halved
125 g/4 oz raspberries
2 tbsp Grand Marnier
  or Cointreau
8–10 medium slices white bread,
  crusts removed
mint sprigs, to decorate
low-fat Greek-set yogurt or
  low-fat fromage frais,
  to serve

## Step-by-step guide

1  Place the redcurrants, sugar
   and 1 tablespoon of water in a
   large saucepan. Heat gently until
   the sugar has just dissolved and
   the juices have just begun to run.

2  Remove the saucepan from the
   heat and stir in the strawberries,
   raspberries and the Grand
   Marnier or Cointreau.

3  Line the base and sides of
   a 1.1 litre/2 pint pudding basin
   with two thirds of the bread,
   making sure that the slices
   overlap each other slightly.

4  Spoon the fruit with their juices
   into the bread-lined pudding
   basin, then top with the remaining
   bread slices.

5  Place a small plate on top of the
   pudding inside the pudding basin.
   Ensure the plate fits tightly, then
   weigh down with a clean can or
   some weights and chill in the
   refrigerator overnight.

6  When ready to serve, remove the
   weights and plate. Carefully
   loosen round the sides of the
   basin with a round-bladed knife.
   Invert the pudding on to a serving
   plate, decorate with the mint
   sprigs and serve with the yogurt
   or fromage frais.

cows' milk-free   egg-free   gluten-free   wheat-free   nut-free   vegetarian   vegan   seafood-free